CyberGeek® is

Paul Zurlini & Richard Flammer

Illustrations by Paul Zurlini

www.cybergeek.com

CCC Publications
Chatsworth, California

Published by

CCC Publications
9725 Lurline Avenue
Chatsworth, CA 91311

Manufactured in the United States of America

Cover ©1998 CCC Publications

Interior illustrations ©1998 CCC Publications

Cover & interior art by Paul Zurlini

Cover/Interior production by Oasis Graphics

ISBN: 1-57644-080-X

If your local U.S. bookstore is out of stock, copies of this book may be obtained by mailing check or money order for $6.95 per book (plus $3.00 to cover postage and handling) to: "Order Dept." at the above address.

Pre-publication Edition – 1/99

Acknowledgements

The authors wish to thank the following people for
conceptual, literary and emotional support:

Mom & Dad Flammer
Mom & Dad Zurlini
Mary Maidens
Mala Rajan
Macintosh
Ster
Mokey
Maggie
Shelly the Bartender
&
my wife, Keri, for being there even when she wasn't.

Thanks.

INTRODUCTION

How long will you allow yourself to be mislabeled? You're a CYBERgeek, but your friends may call you a geek. Potsie was a geek. Do you dress or act like Potsie? Donnie and Marie are geeks. Would you listen to their music? Barry Manilow, Erkle, Richard Simmons... the list goes on and on. Geeks!

Do you belong in the geek category? If you're standing there reading this in tight polyester slacks and penny loafers, have recently attended and enjoyed a John Tesh concert and think Spam has only one meaning and that it makes a darn good meal: you're probably a geek. Close this book and go look for one more suitable to your tastes in the section marked "New Age Living," "Birdwatching," or "Interior Floral Design."

If your computer work station looks like a carnival at night, you possess a sense of style beyond the comprehension of your peers,

and you've actually scored in a chat room, hoorah for you! You're a
CYBERgeek! A member in good sitting of Generation Tech.

    A trend-setting, cyber-cruising inhabitant of the planet Earth,
destined to be part of an amazing revolution in the development and
exchange of knowledge and ideas. You're smart, hip, slightly
off-center and online near the cutting edge of the world.

    Congratulations! You're a CYBERgeek. Don't let them call you a
geek. They may be a *geek*. But you're a CYBERgeek. Still need more
clarification? Read on...

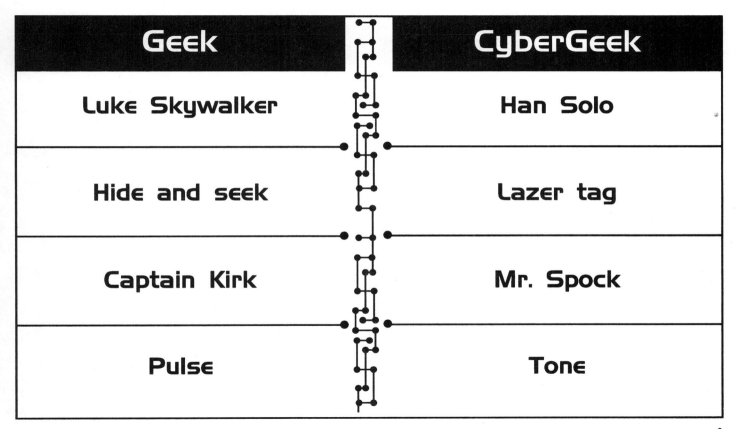

Geek	CyberGeek
Luke Skywalker	Han Solo
Hide and seek	Lazer tag
Captain Kirk	Mr. Spock
Pulse	Tone

I

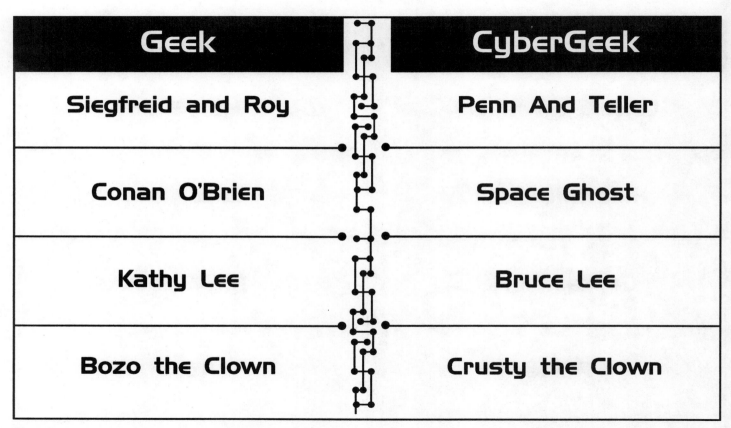

Geek	CyberGeek
Siegfreid and Roy	Penn And Teller
Conan O'Brien	Space Ghost
Kathy Lee	Bruce Lee
Bozo the Clown	Crusty the Clown

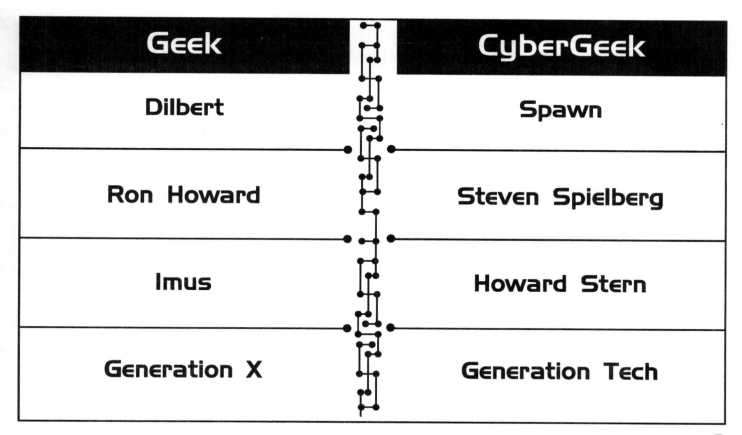

Geek	CyberGeek
Dilbert	Spawn
Ron Howard	Steven Spielberg
Imus	Howard Stern
Generation X	Generation Tech

3

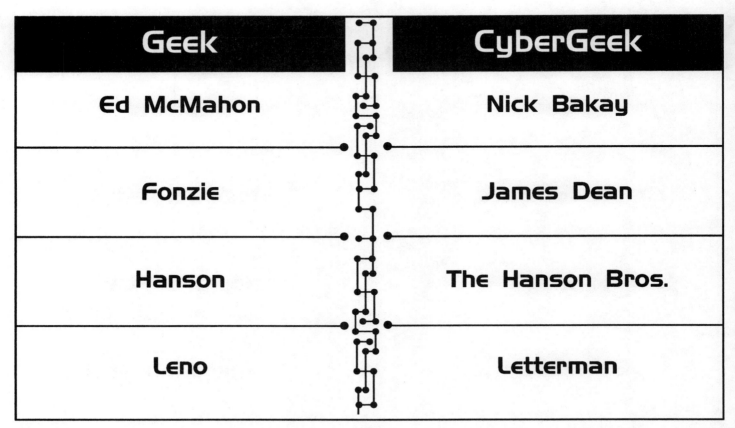

Geek	CyberGeek
Ed McMahon	Nick Bakay
Fonzie	James Dean
Hanson	The Hanson Bros.
Leno	Letterman

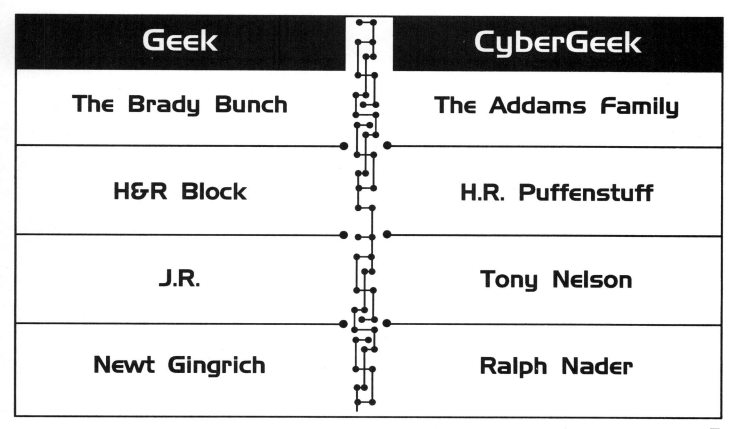

Geek	CyberGeek
The Brady Bunch	The Addams Family
H&R Block	H.R. Puffenstuff
J.R.	Tony Nelson
Newt Gingrich	Ralph Nader

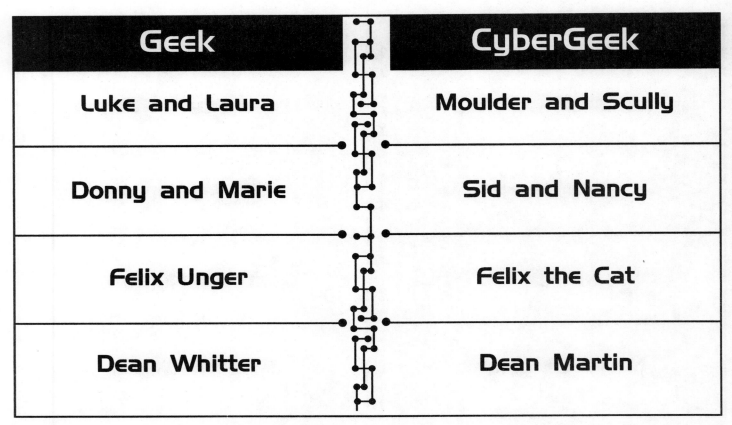

Geek	CyberGeek
Luke and Laura	Moulder and Scully
Donny and Marie	Sid and Nancy
Felix Unger	Felix the Cat
Dean Whitter	Dean Martin

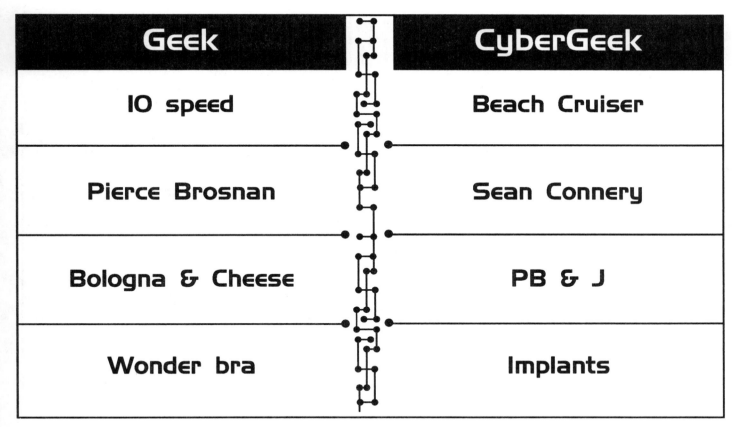

Geek	CyberGeek
10 speed	Beach Cruiser
Pierce Brosnan	Sean Connery
Bologna & Cheese	PB & J
Wonder bra	Implants

7

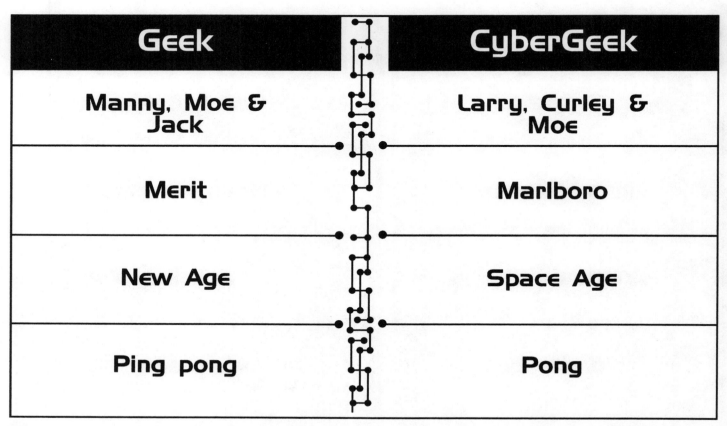

Geek	CyberGeek
Manny, Moe & Jack	Larry, Curley & Moe
Merit	Marlboro
New Age	Space Age
Ping pong	Pong

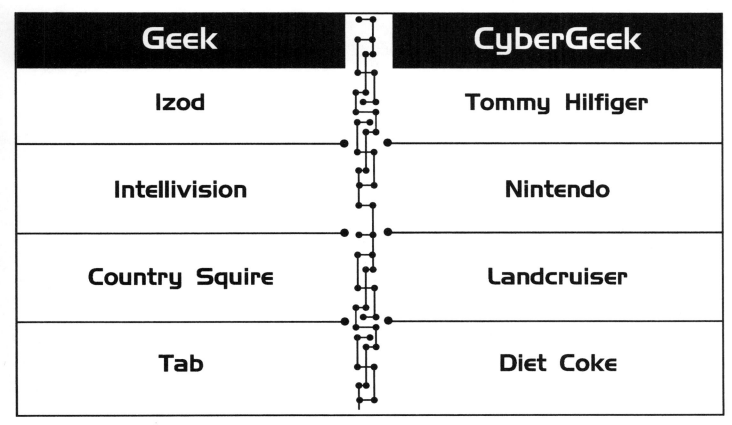

Geek	CyberGeek
Izod	Tommy Hilfiger
Intellivision	Nintendo
Country Squire	Landcruiser
Tab	Diet Coke

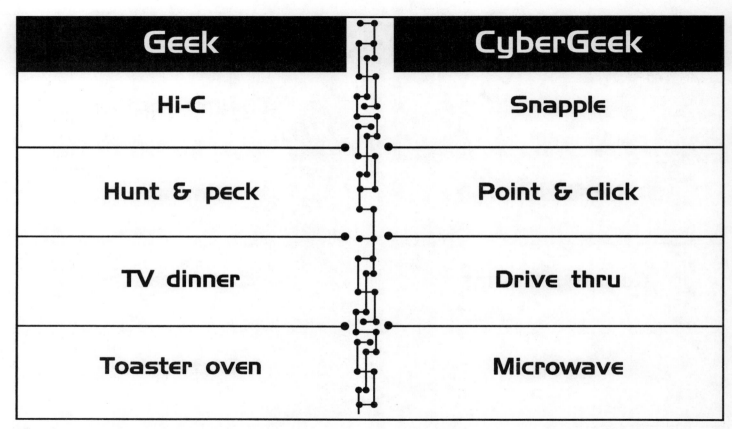

Geek	CyberGeek
Hi-C	Snapple
Hunt & peck	Point & click
TV dinner	Drive thru
Toaster oven	Microwave

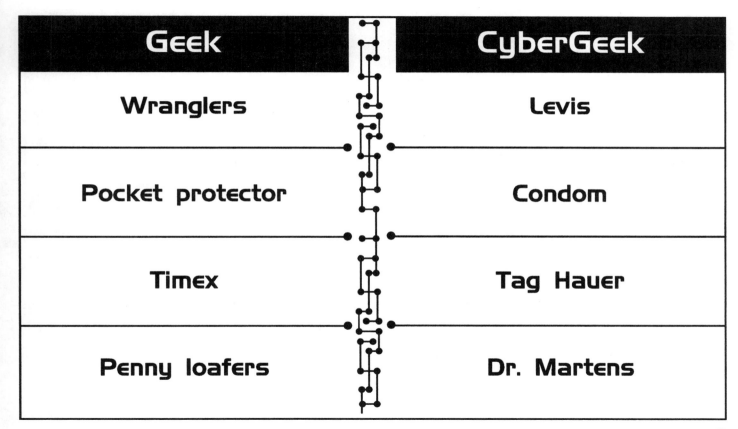

Geek	CyberGeek
Wranglers	Levis
Pocket protector	Condom
Timex	Tag Hauer
Penny loafers	Dr. Martens

II

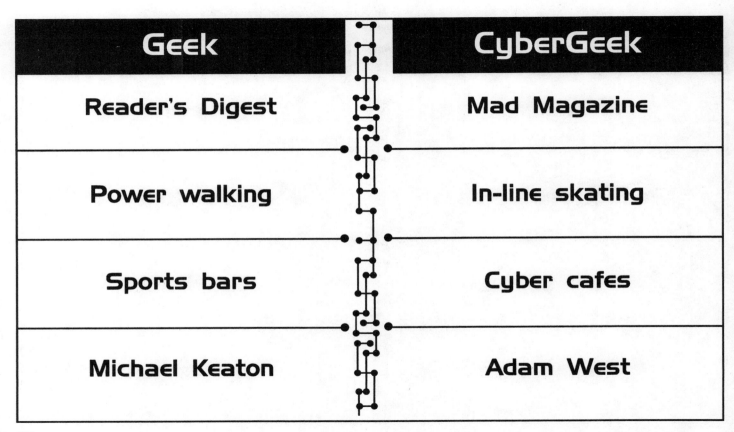

Geek	CyberGeek
Reader's Digest	Mad Magazine
Power walking	In-line skating
Sports bars	Cyber cafes
Michael Keaton	Adam West

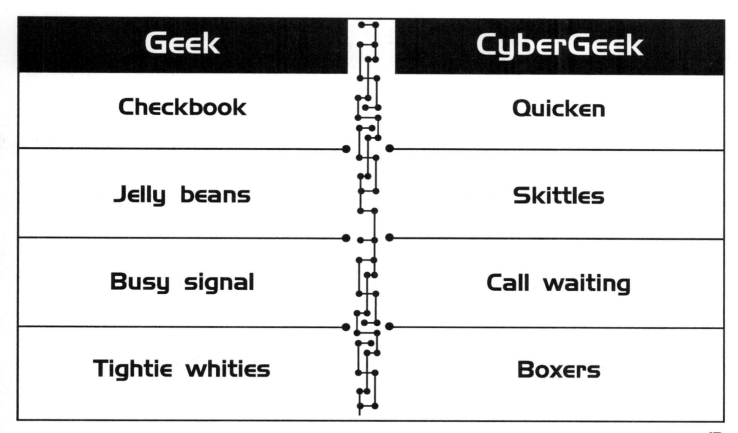

Geek	CyberGeek
Checkbook	Quicken
Jelly beans	Skittles
Busy signal	Call waiting
Tightie whities	Boxers

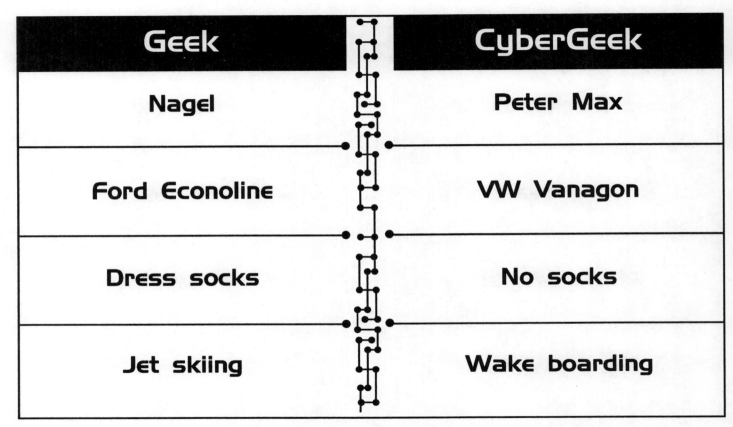

Geek	CyberGeek
Nagel	Peter Max
Ford Econoline	VW Vanagon
Dress socks	No socks
Jet skiing	Wake boarding

Geek	CyberGeek
Sea Breeze	Martini
Pomade	Gel
Breyers	Ben and Jerry's
Keds	Vans

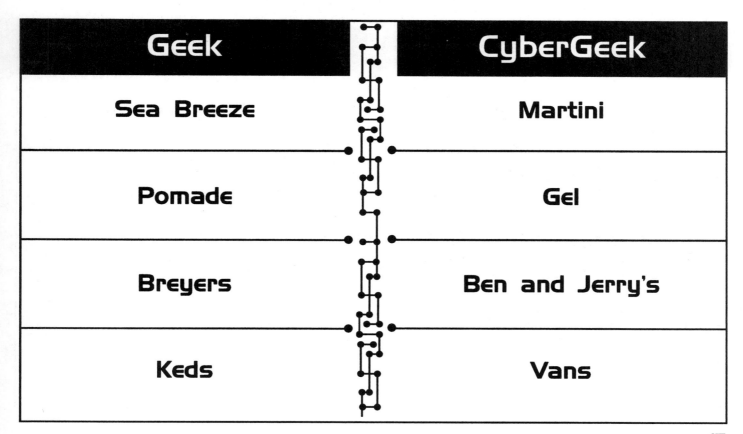

15

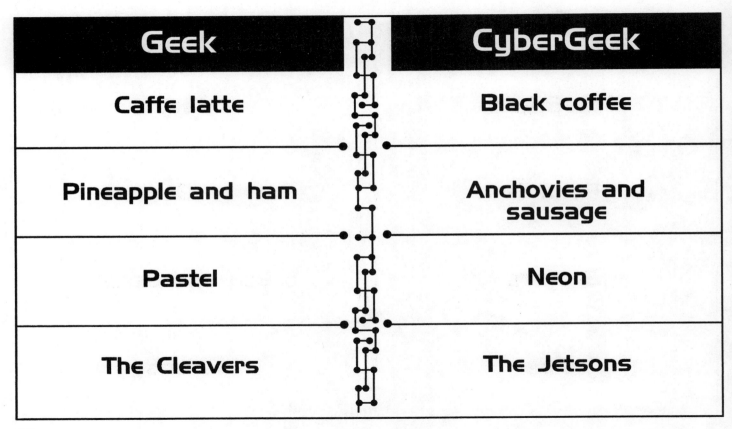

Geek	CyberGeek
Caffe latte	Black coffee
Pineapple and ham	Anchovies and sausage
Pastel	Neon
The Cleavers	The Jetsons

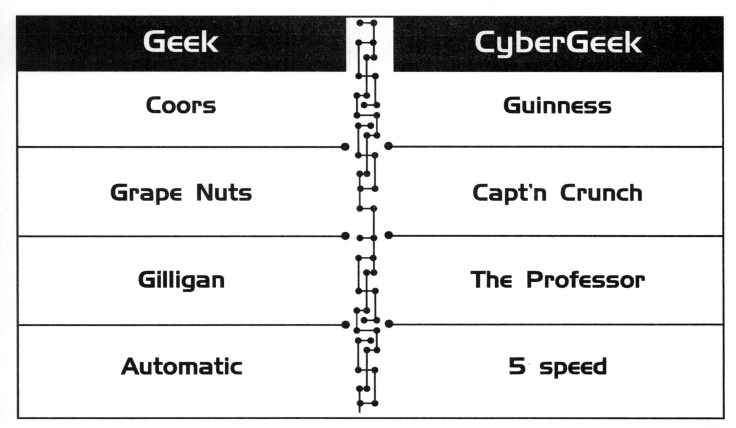

Geek	CyberGeek
Coors	Guinness
Grape Nuts	Capt'n Crunch
Gilligan	The Professor
Automatic	5 speed

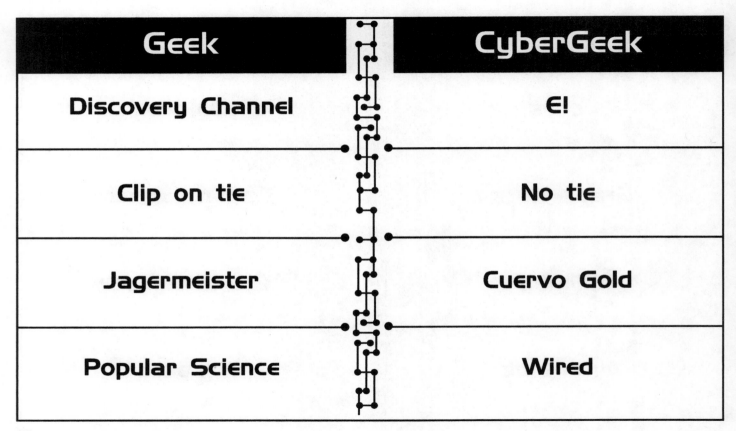

Geek	CyberGeek
Discovery Channel	E!
Clip on tie	No tie
Jagermeister	Cuervo Gold
Popular Science	Wired

18

you've tried to create an emoticon in your own likeness.

You're most likely a CyberGeek if...

you monitor the severity of your acne by calculating dots per inch.

you've taken your laptop computer into a coffee shop to pick-up girls.

you've invited a friend over to "interface."

You're most likely a CyberGeek if...

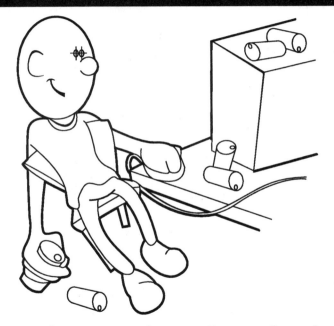

you've ever logged on drunk.

You're most likely a CyberGeek if...

your spouse is jealous of your computer.

you've used a word processing program
to create a simple grocery list.

you brag @ parties about your carpal
tunnel syndrome.

you keep your screen saver on because the girl in the next cubicle thinks flying toasters are cute.

You're most likely a CyberGeek if...

you've ever been called a "social idiot."

you advise two friends that just broke up to try a "restart.".

you consider yourself a designer because you have the latest version of CorelDraw.

You're most likely a CyberGeek if...

you brag about your "memory" but often
forget what day it is.

you're often caught surfing the
web @ work.

your conversations start with "how's your
system running?," not "how's the family?"

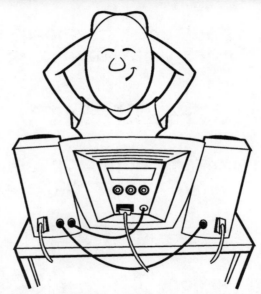

you keep your speaker volume on high because the squeal of a modem inspires you.

You're most likely a CyberGeek if...

you would rather light your hair on fire
and put it out with a hammer than
call tech support.

you considered "Pong" a sport as a kid.

the words "micro" and "soft" no longer
offend your manhood.

You're most likely a CyberGeek if...

you decorate your Christmas tree with old shareware CD's.

You're most likely a CyberGeek if...

you recite the end of the alphabet:
"QRSTWWW.XYZ"

you are trying to get reimbursed for all the mileage you've done on the information superhighway.

after a lengthy web surfing session, you realize you've been wearing the same clothes for more than two days.

You're most likely a CyberGeek if...

you've ever shown anyone older than you how to use a computer.

You're most likely a CyberGeek if...

you consider "Area 51" as a possible honeymoon destination.

you know what "HTML" stands for.

you log car mileage on a spread sheet to figure out how many MPG's your car really gets.

You're most likely a CyberGeek if...

**fast food containers are an integral part
of your desktop layout.**

You're most likely a CyberGeek if...

you've forgotten how to write with a pen.

you fix your hair and put on make-up
before you visit the internet mall.

you go months without using a
postage stamp.

You're most likely a CyberGeek if...

your friends have your number listed
under "Tech Support."

you try not to snicker as you ask your
friend: "that's your computer?"

you got so drunk on New Year's Eve
your "resolution" was reduced to 100 DPI.

You're most likely a CyberGeek if...

your taboo topics for discussion include
politics, religion and Mac vs. PC.

you quickly find out the reason you've
been invited over to a friend's house is to
program an electronic device.

you're currently "dating" someone you
haven't actually met.

You're most likely a CyberGeek if...

your computer system is worth more
than your car and approaching the value
of your home.

you've gone to hit the undo key after
making a mistake, and realized you were
not anywhere near a computer.

no matter how cold you get, you refuse
to close windows.

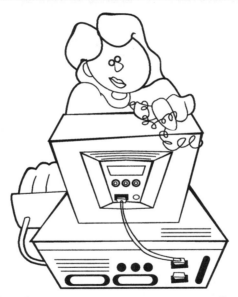

you need to turn on your computer to find a friend's phone number.

You're most likely a CyberGeek if...

you know as many acronyms as an
engineer @ NASA.

your favorite 3 letters of the
alphabet are WWW

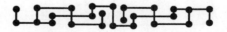

you've named your son Earl and your
daughter Dot.

You're most likely a CyberGeek if...

you dream in programmer's code.

You're most likely a CyberGeek if...

you've made fun of your friends'
modem speed.

you have never paid for software.

you've ever collected ALL of the free pins
@ a computer trade show.

You're most likely a CyberGeek if...

you laughed @ jocks in High School because you knew after college YOU'D have the Porsche and babes.

You're most likely a CyberGeek if...

you turn on your computer more often
than your partner.

you'd rather have a fast modem
than a fast car.

you have ever called someone a "newbie."

you consider your laptop a fashion accessory.

You're most likely a CyberGeek if...

you frequently fly your own private jet to the Bahamas...until your spouse yells @ you to turn off the flight simulator.

you spend more money on RAM than you do on your mate.

you can use "Spam" as a verb in a sentence.

you have more than one T-shirt with a computer logo on it.

The word "dude" has become a staple of your E-mail vocabulary.

you dream of meeting your soulmate @ CompUSA.

You're most likely a CyberGeek if...

once you got your computer out safely, you returned to your burning house to save your wife.

You're most likely a CyberGeek if...

you've felt an uncontrollable wave of coolness after you're asked to turn on your laptop for airport security.

you can shoot below par on computer golf.

you have ever sent a fax or E-mail from an airplane.

You're most likely a CyberGeek if...

your CPU gets hot enough to fry an egg on it.

You're most likely a CyberGeek if...

your office is lit-up like
Las Vegas @ night.

you h/v no difficulty//:reading.thissentence

you've personally tested all of your
appliances for Year 2000 compliance.

You're most likely a CyberGeek if...

you've decided to take the money you spend on make-up and
upgrade your computer so you can get more dates.

You're most likely a CyberGeek if...

your kids need to log-on when you tell
them to go play with their friends.

all you have on your
Christmas list is software.

you've encouraged all of your friends and
family to buy computers so you no longer
have to hand-write letters.

you wish you could use a virus detection
software on your new boyfriend.

You're most likely a CyberGeek if...

you would rather cruise the web for prospective dates than go out to bars.

you think "hair extensions" are part of a beauty salon software.

you even plug your blender and crock pot into a surge protector.

You're most likely a CyberGeek if...

you just might say to an intruder in your home: "Do what you want to my family but please don't hurt my computer!"

you've asked the valet at a fancy hotel where you should go to "log in."

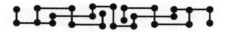

you think "dinnerware" is a recipe program.

You're most likely a CyberGeek if...

you wisely chose computer programming
over woodshop in high school.

you have @ least one pet named "Bill."

when the elevator doors don't close, you
tell the person closest to the buttons:
"Press any key to continue."

you've critiqued the program design of your local ATM.

you haven't bought floppies in the last 5 years because AOL mails them to you everyday for free.

you call a thrift-shop flannel shirt and a pair of sweat pants an "outfit."

you've stayed home from work to take care of your computer when it had a virus.

you can immediately identify any font
by size and name.

you have every episode of the
X-files on video.

you've used software to track your diet.

you wish 7-11 sold floppies so you could buy them with your coffee and cigs.

You're most likely a CyberGeek if...

you collect Star Wars, Spawn or
Star Trek memorabilia.

you've had to explain to your friends who
"Hal" is & how they arrived @ his name.

you change your screen saver more often
than you change your underwear.

You're most likely a CyberGeek if...

you consider the fish on your screen-saver as pets.

You're most likely a CyberGeek if...

online dating has made you incredibly
proficient @ typing with one hand.

you've described a colorblind friend as
"only being able to see in gray scale."

you wish the same pick-up lines that
worked in chat rooms also
worked in person.

You're most likely a CyberGeek if...

you would rather party with **Bill Gates** and **Steve Jobs** than **Cindy Crawford** and **Tira Banks**.

You're most likely a CyberGeek if...

you've ever used the excuse "My hard drive ate my homework."

your blood type is "french roast."

you measure the size of a meal in bytes.

you've ever been abducted.

You're most likely a CyberGeek if...

you believe toasters can really fly.

you're sure there's a software problem
when you get home and there's no
E-mail for you.

Bill Gates frequently appears in your
dreams *and* nightmares.

you made your first million before you lost your virginity.

you thought the most exciting part of the movie "The Net" was picking out the inconsistencies.

you've advised your kid not to play on a sports team because it would interfere with computer programming classes.

You're most likely a CyberGeek if...

you wish you could buy memory @ your local hardware store and RAM @ the butcher shop.

you not only read unsolicited E-mail, you actually enjoy getting it.

you check your E-mail more often than you check on your infant.

You're most likely a CyberGeek if...

you've downloaded pictures of
questionable taste on to your hard drive.

You're most likely a CyberGeek if...

you and your fiance registered
for wedding gifts @ Egghead Software.

when you see a mouse you quickly
jump into a chair.

you consider being called "anti-social"
a compliment.

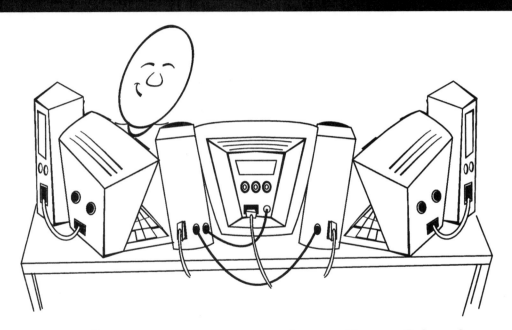

you have more computers than friends.

You're most likely a CyberGeek if...

you own @ least one Jerry Garcia necktie.

your coffee pot is set to go off 10 minutes before your computer is.

you describe the pain encountered @ the dentist in units of "megahertz."

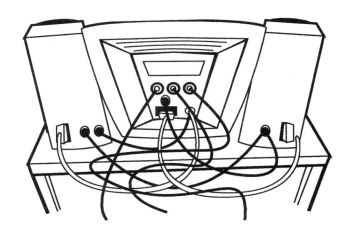

the cables behind your computer look like an
explosion @ a spaghetti factory.

You're most likely a CyberGeek if...

you proudly display your free America
Online disk collection as if you're the only
one who has one.

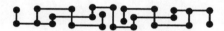

your hair frequently looks uncombed and
messy because your hair is frequently
uncombed and messy.

you think "Big Mac" means a
300 MHz Apple computer.

you wish you had access to the "escape" key
after meeting your blind date.

You're most likely a CyberGeek if...

you've mentally re-designed the layout and graphics on take-out food flyers left in your mailbox.

you only hang around with people you "click" with.

you frequently incorporate emoticons into your handwritten letters :)

you've posted a guard dog @ your computer so your family won't go near it.

You're most likely a CyberGeek if...

you have taken the batteries out of your emergency flashlight to use in your PDA.

you got a dog just so you could name him "Browser."

you refer to eating as "downloading food files."

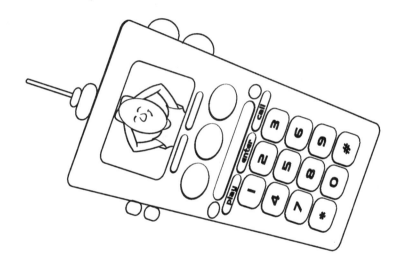

you have one device that operates as a phone, fax, pager, e-mailer, TV remote, electric shaver, egg-timer and PDA.

You're most likely a CyberGeek if...

lately you've been too busy
creating your personal web page to
notice the opposite sex.

after meeting your family and friends, you
happily report to your fiance that he/she
is compatible with your network.

your perfect mate is "PC," "portable,"
"voice activated," "user friendly"
and "ergonomic."

TITLES BY CCC PUBLICATIONS

Blank Books ($3.99)
SEX AFTER BABY
SEX AFTER 30
SEX AFTER 40
SEX AFTER 50

Retail $4.95 – $4.99
30 – DEAL WITH IT!
40 – DEAL WITH IT!
50 – DEAL WITH IT!
60 – DEAL WITH IT!
RETIRED – DEAL WITH IT!
OVER THE HILL – DEAL WITH IT!
"?" book
POSITIVELY PREGNANT
CAN SEX IMPROVE YOUR GOLF?
THE COMPLETE BOOGER BOOK
FLYING FUNNIES
MARITAL BLISS & OXYMORONS
THE VERY VERY SEXY ADULT DOT-TO-DOT BOOK
THE DEFINITIVE FART BOOK
THE COMPLETE WIMP'S GUIDE TO SEX
THE CAT OWNER'S SHAPE UP MANUAL
THE OFFICE FROM HELL
FITNESS FANATICS
YOUNGER MEN ARE BETTER THAN RETIN-A
BUT OSSIFER, IT'S NOT MY FAULT
YOU KNOW YOU'RE AN OLD FART WHEN...
1001 WAYS TO PROCRASTINATE
HORMONES FROM HELL II
SHARING THE ROAD WITH IDIOTS
THE GREATEST ANSWERING MACHINE MESSAGES
WHAT DO WE DO NOW??
HOW TO TALK YOU WAY OUT OF A TRAFFIC TICKET
THE BOTTOM HALF

LIFE'S MOST EMBARRASSING MOMENTS
HOW TO ENTERTAIN PEOPLE YOU HATE
YOUR GUIDE TO CORPORATE SURVIVAL
THE SUPERIOR PERSON'S GUIDE
GIFTING RIGHT
NO HANG-UPS (Volumes I, II & III – $3.95 ea.)
TOTALLY OUTRAGEOUS BUMPER-SNICKERS ($2.95)

Retail $5.95
SINGLE WOMEN VS. MARRIED WOMEN
TAKE A WOMAN'S WORD FOR IT
SEXY CROTCHWORD PUZZLES
SO, YOU'RE GETTING MARRIED
YOU KNOW HE'S A WOMANIZING SLIMEBALL WHEN...
GETTING OLD SUCKS
WHY GOD MAKES BALD GUYS
OH BABY!
PMS CRAZED: TOUCH ME AND I'LL KILL YOU!
OVER THE HILL – DEAL WITH IT!
WHY MEN ARE CLUELESS
THE BOOK OF WHITE TRASH
THE ART OF MOONING
GOLFAHOLICS
CRINKLED 'N' WRINKLED
SMART COMEBACKS FOR STUPID QUESTIONS
YIKES! IT'S ANOTHER BIRTHDAY
SEX IS A GAME
SEX AND YOUR STARS
SIGNS YOUR SEX LIFE IS DEAD
40 AND HOLDING YOUR OWN
50 AND HOLDING YOUR OWN
MALE BASHING: WOMEN'S FAVORITE PASTIME
THINGS YOU CAN DO WITH A USELESS MAN
MORE THINGS YOU CAN DO WITH A USELESS MAN
RETIREMENT: THE GET EVEN YEARS

THE WORLD'S GREATEST PUT-DOWN LINES
LITTLE INSTRUCTION BOOK OF THE RICH & FAMOUS
WELCOME TO YOUR MIDLIFE CRISIS
GETTING EVEN WITH THE ANSWERING MACHINE
ARE YOU A SPORTS NUT?
MEN ARE PIGS / WOMEN ARE BITCHES
THE BETTER HALF
ARE WE DYSFUNCTIONAL YET?
TECHNOLOGY BYTES!
50 WAYS TO HUSTLE YOUR FRIENDS
HORMONES FROM HELL
HUSBANDS FROM HELL
KILLER BRAS & Other Hazards Of The 50's
IT'S BETTER TO BE OVER THE HILL THAN UNDER IT
HOW TO REALLY PARTY!!!
WORK SUCKS!
THE PEOPLE WATCHER'S FIELD GUIDE
THE ABSOLUTE LAST CHANCE DIET BOOK
FOR MEN ONLY (How To Survive Marriage)
THE UGLY TRUTH ABOUT MEN
NEVER A DULL CARD
THE LITTLE BOOK OF ROMANTIC LIES
IT'S A MAD MAD MAD SPORTS WORLD ($6.95)
THE LITTLE BOOK OF CORPORATE LIES ($6.95)
RED HOT MONOGAMY ($6.95)
LOVE DAT CAT ($6.95)
HOW TO SURVIVE A JEWISH MOTHER ($6.95)
WHY MEN DON'T HAVE A CLUE ($7.99)
LADIES, START YOUR ENGINES! ($7.99)

NO HANG-UPS – CASSETTES Retail $5.98
Vol. I:	GENERAL MESSAGES (M or F)	
Vol. II:	BUSINESS MESSAGES (M or F)	
Vol. III:	'R' RATED MESSAGES (M or F)	
Vol. V:	CELEBRI-TEASE